READING WITH ANIMAL MINI-BOOKS

READING WITH ANIMAL MINI-BOOKS

Learn to Read and Write with Rhyming Word Families

Celeste Meiergerd

ULYSSES PRESS

Published in the United States by:
Ulysses Press
PO Box 3440
Berkeley, CA 94703
www.ulyssespress.com

ISBN: 978-1-64604-253-1
Library of Congress Control Number: 2021937753

Printed in the United States by Kingery Printing Company
10 9 8 7 6 5 4 3 2 1

Acquisitions editor: Casie Vogel
Managing editor: Claire Chun
Editor: Pat Harris
Proofreader: Joyce Wu
Front cover design: Jake Flaherty
Interior design: what!design @ whatweb.com and Jake Flaherty
Production: Jake Flaherty
Cover art: tiger © GraphicsRF.com/shutterstock.com; giraffe © White Space Illustrations/shutterstock.com
Interior art: shutterstock.com

CONTENTS

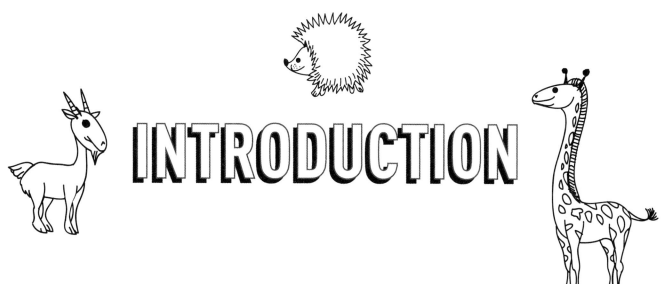

INTRODUCTION

What to Expect in This Workbook

Encourage early reading and writing skills as well as recognition of different word families among your young learners with the *Reading with Animal Mini-Books* workbook! *Reading with Animal Mini-Books* is a workbook full of removable mini-books ready to be carefully crafted by children and students ranging from preschool to first grade. All of the mini-books center on the practice of essential early literacy skills through reading and writing familiar sight words in basic word families. The stories emphasize the use of simple CVC (consonant, vowel, consonant) words, such as "cat" and "map," to make them applicable for the earliest readers. As the workbook advances from mini-book to mini-book, the complexity of the word families and the words used in the stories increase in difficulty as well. This slow buildup allows for the greatest chance of success among the intended ages, as well as ease for an adult to find the perfect mini-book at the desired level.

The Importance of Learning through Word Families

Children learn through exposure and repetition. This is why they can "read" familiar brands while walking through the grocery store or understand an advertisement in a magazine before they even know their letter sounds. When the use of word families is incorporated into early reading practice, children are more likely to recognize and recall what particular word endings look and sound like.

When reading, if children are able to recall an ending sound, it is much easier for them to sound out a potential new word, as they have to sound out only the beginning part of the word. As they see the similar word endings within the stories in these mini-books, they will begin to make connections to how the words are read.

What Makes This Workbook Special

This workbook is perfect for early readers because of its repetitive nature. The mini-books are similar in the way they progress, with each page building on the previous one. This allows the young readers to really understand what each word is before seeing a new word appear. Unlike flash cards, which can be dull for a young child, this workbook provides repetition in a fun and engaging way.

Each page includes young children's favorite animals and memorable rhymes that make reading fun and interesting. The rhyming scheme on each page makes the reading feel lyrical—allowing for children to begin recognizing which sounds different letter combinations make in each word. With over thirty unique mini-books ready to be made, and each page featuring young children's favorite animals acting out silly scenes, the learning of each word family is distinct and unforgettable. The black-and-white pages invite young children to color, write, and read their very own mini-book creations, allowing them to be in control of their own learning with the ability to create.

Additionally, the activities woven into the mini-books provide enough instruction for children to maintain accuracy in the content they're learning and achieving. Traceable letters with exact sizing and fill-in-the-blank letters for words previously seen in a story allow for higher chances of success for every child at every reading level. Children are gifted with the opportunity to feel that they are writing their own stories and to feel success when they see it all come together with that special touch of their favorite colors and their own handwriting. Once the mini-book is filled in and ready to read, the pictures on the pages will provide context clues that allow young readers to strive toward successful, independent reading.

How to Use This Workbook

The format of this workbook leaves lots of room for flexibility in the way it is presented. The mini-books can be made by the specifications listed here: perfectly torn out, bound together, and ready to be filled in by a child with guidance, making use of favorite crayons, pencils, and markers. Or, for more advanced learners, children can be encouraged to independently write, tear, and put together their own books.

These mini-books focus on numerous basic word families and are applicable for working with an individual child or can be copied for multiple students' use. Although this workbook emphasizes children's independence and self-confidence in their reading and writing skills, having an adult as part of their experience can make a dramatic impact on how successful they are. This workbook is a great fit for both the prepared parent and the knowledgeable teacher, both striving to enrich a child's learning to prepare for those first days of school and to spark creativity in the way students transition to independent readers.

Time to get started. Let's make some books!

How to Put the Mini-Books Together

The pages in the *Reading with Animal Mini-Books* workbook include perforated edges for easy removal without any content being left behind through rips or tears. Putting each mini-book together is so simple with the help of the built-in perforated edges. These perforations are along each page of the mini-books and also along the overall binding of the entire workbook. The ease of these perforations allows for quick setup and removes the need for scissors! Here are the steps for making perfect mini-books every time:

- Simply tear out the sheet containing the book you want. Be sure to rip at the perforated edge located in the center of the book.

If you want to have multiple copies of a mini-book (for classroom use or otherwise), make a double-sided copy before going on to the next step.

Front   Back

• Next, look for the perforated edge that separates the pages of the mini-book (if you are looking at the cover page, the perforated edge will split pages 5 and 8 as well as page 4 and the cover page). Rip along this perforated edge so that you have two separate sheets of paper.

Tear in half at the perforation

- Lay the pages on top of each other so that page 4 and 5 is on top of page 2 and 7.

- Line up these two papers so that they are even, and then fold in half along the middle seam of the pages so that the cover ends up facing you.

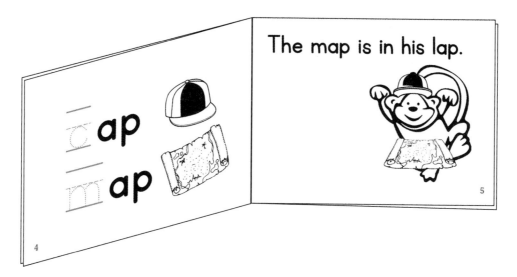

- Now you can bind the pages together. There are many ways to do this, but here are a few ideas:

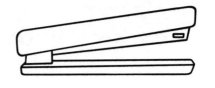

  * Staple the pages together.

  * Hole punch the corner of the pages and have the child choose a special color of ribbon or yarn to tie the pages together.

  * Put brass tacks on the side for more movement of the pages.

  * The possibilities for binding are endless! Include children in the process to have them even more excited about creating their mini-books.

- And finally...it's done! The mini-book is ready to use.

Monkey and the Map

1

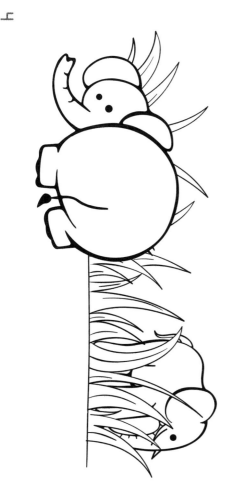

The lad looks for Dad.

The
Dad

Is Dad mad?

-ad Word Practice

___ ad

___ ad

___ ad

l	s	p

l

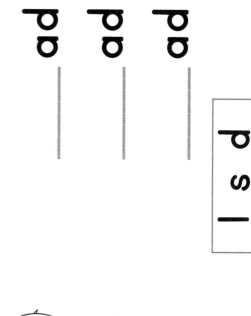

Where is Dad?

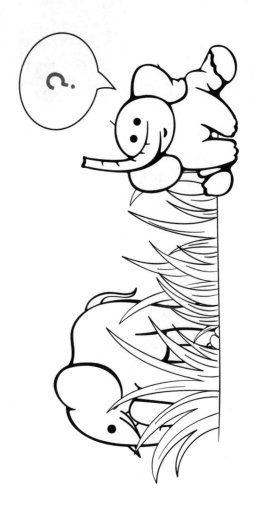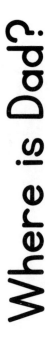

Is Dad sad?

Here is the lad.

No, Dad is glad!

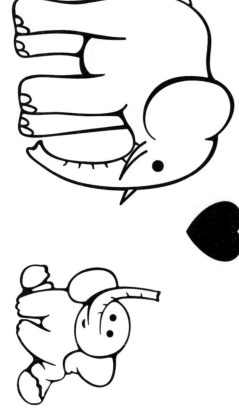

_ag

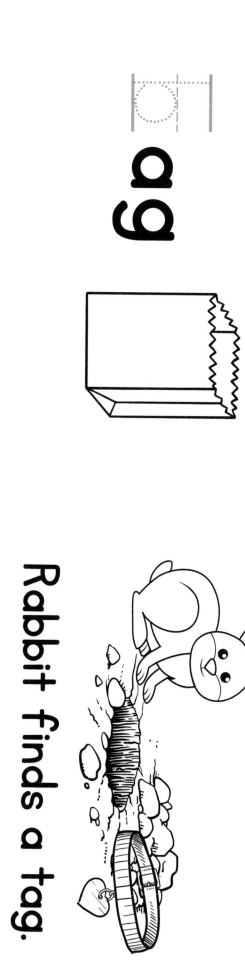

Rabbit Digs

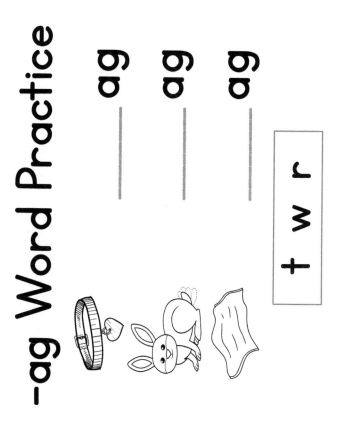

Rabbit finds a tag.

-ag Word Practice

___ ag

___ ag

___ ag

t w r

Rabbit puts
it in the bag.

Rabbit finds a rag.

Rabbit puts
it in the bag.

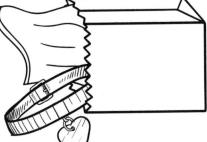

Rabbit's tail
starts to wag.

Ｒ am

Ｓ am

Sam
the Ram

Sam likes ham.

-am Word Practice

___ am

___ am

___ am

h j r

Sam is a ram.

Here is Sam.

Sam likes jam.

Sam eats jam on ham.

Dolphin and Dan

Dolphin and Dan
drive in a van.

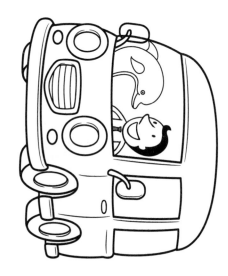

Dolphin and Dan get a tan.

-an Word Practice

an _____

an _____

an _____

| m | v | f |

3

Dan is a man.

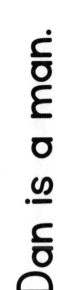

Dolphin is friends with Dan.

Dolphin and Dan ran.

Dolphin and Dan need a fan.

B b

ap

ap

Monkey and the Map

The map is in Monkey's lap.

-ap Word Practice

_____ ap

_____ ap

_____ ap

g c u

g

Monkey finds a map.

Monkey wears a cap.

Monkey sees a gap.

Monkey takes a nap.

z
z z
z

Cat and Rat

This is Rat.

Cat and Rat sat.

-at Word Practice

at _____

at _____

a _____

r c m

This is Cat.

at

at

Cat and Rat sat
on a mat.

That Fat Bat

I see a fat bat.

-at Word Practice

at

at

at

f h b

Ff

at

at

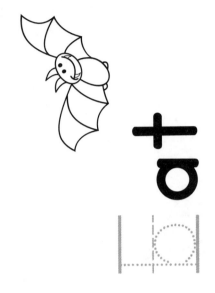

at

I see a bat.

I see a hat.

That fat bat
wears a hat.

Fox finds a sled!

Fox

Fox paints the
sled red.

-ed Word Practice

_____ ed

_____ ed

_____ ed

r b sl

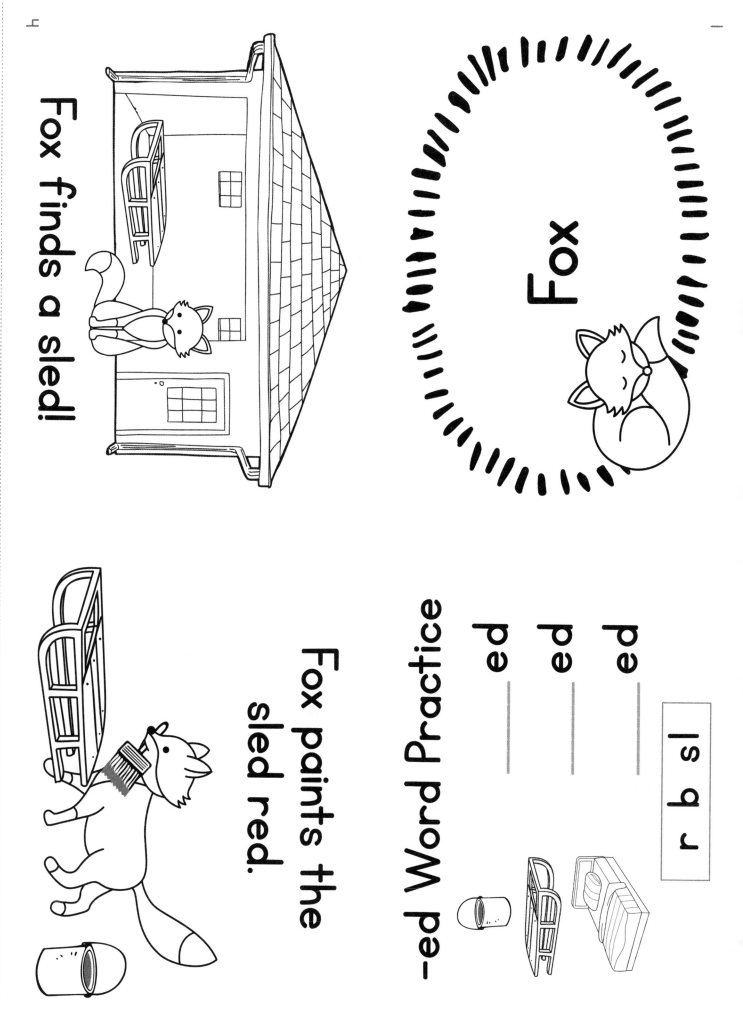

sh e d

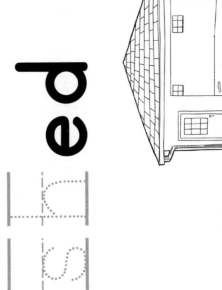

Fox looks in the shed.

Fox rides the red sled.

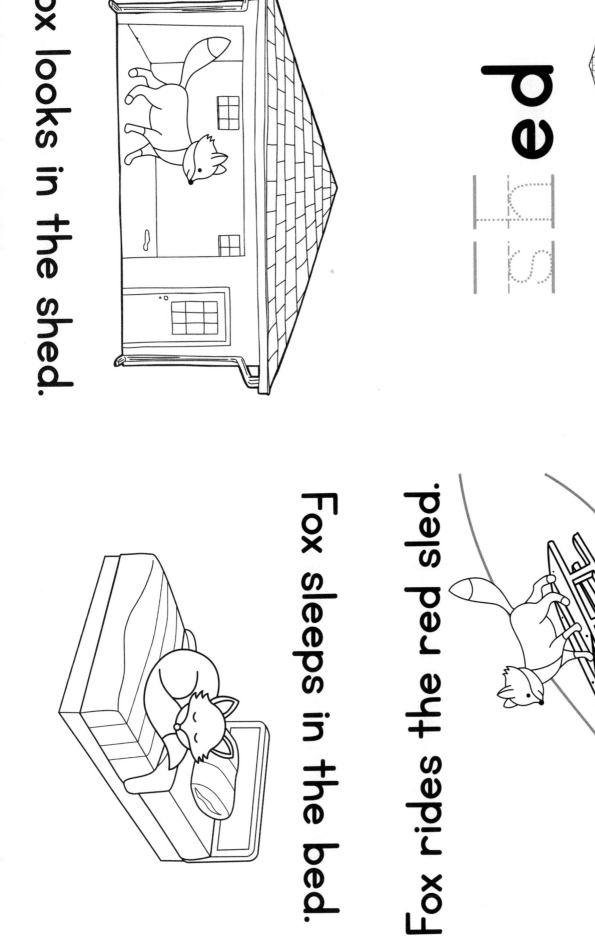

Fox sleeps in the bed.

Inside there is a hen.

Jen sees another hen. Jen counts the hens with a pen.

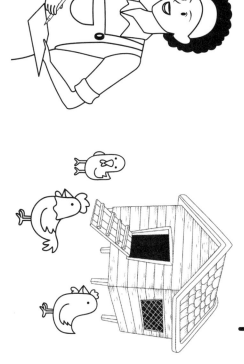

Jen
and the
Ten Hens

-en Word Practice

en ____

en ____

en ____

h p p

Jen opens the den.

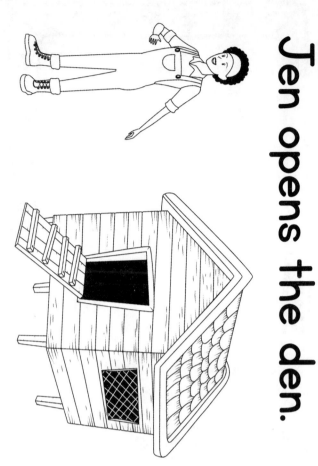

Hen

Ten hens inside the den.

Ten

10

Betty gets
Bird wet.

Betty's
Pet Bird

Betty gets Bird a net.

-et Word Practice

___et

___et

___et

w j n

Bird and Betty met.

Betty gets Bird a jet.

What does
Betty get?

Betty gets a pet!

The big pig will dig.

Pig in a Wig

The big pig
finds a wig.

-ig Word Practice

ig _____

ig _____

ig _____

p   j

big

The pig is big.

wig

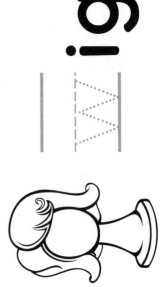

The pig in a wig
does a jig.

They race to the bin.

FINISH

Shark Race

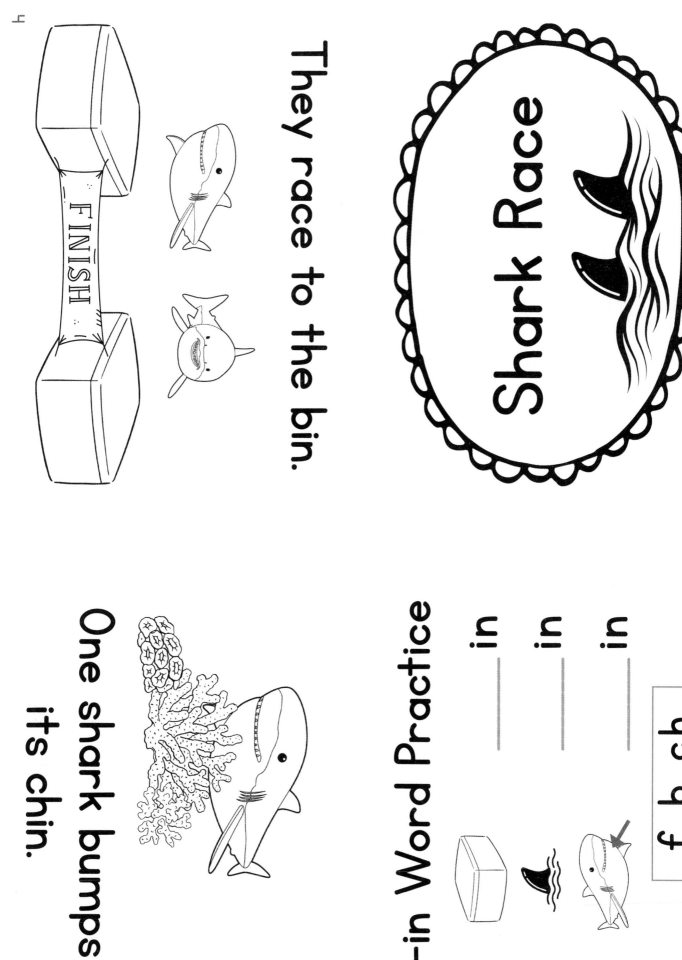

One shark bumps
its chin.

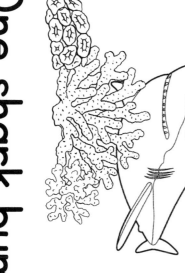

-in Word Practice

u _ in

_ in

_ in

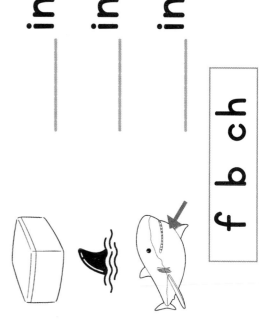

f b ch

Page 2

I see one shark fin.

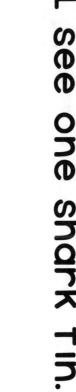

Page 3

I see two.
It is a twin!

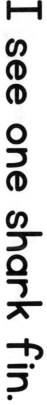

Page 6

Who will win?

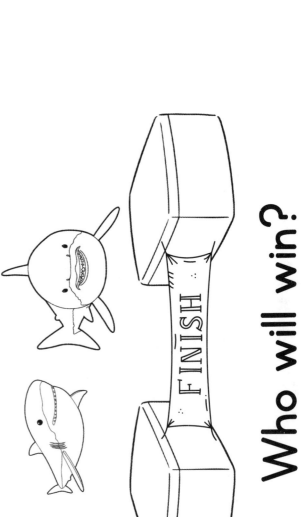

Page 7

win

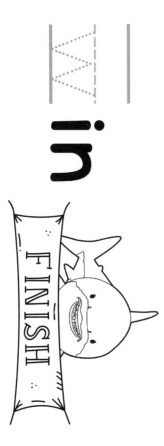

Alligator goes
for a dip.

Alligator
Swim

Alligator puts in the tail's tip.

-ip Word Practice

ip _____

ip _____

ip _____

| l | s | r |

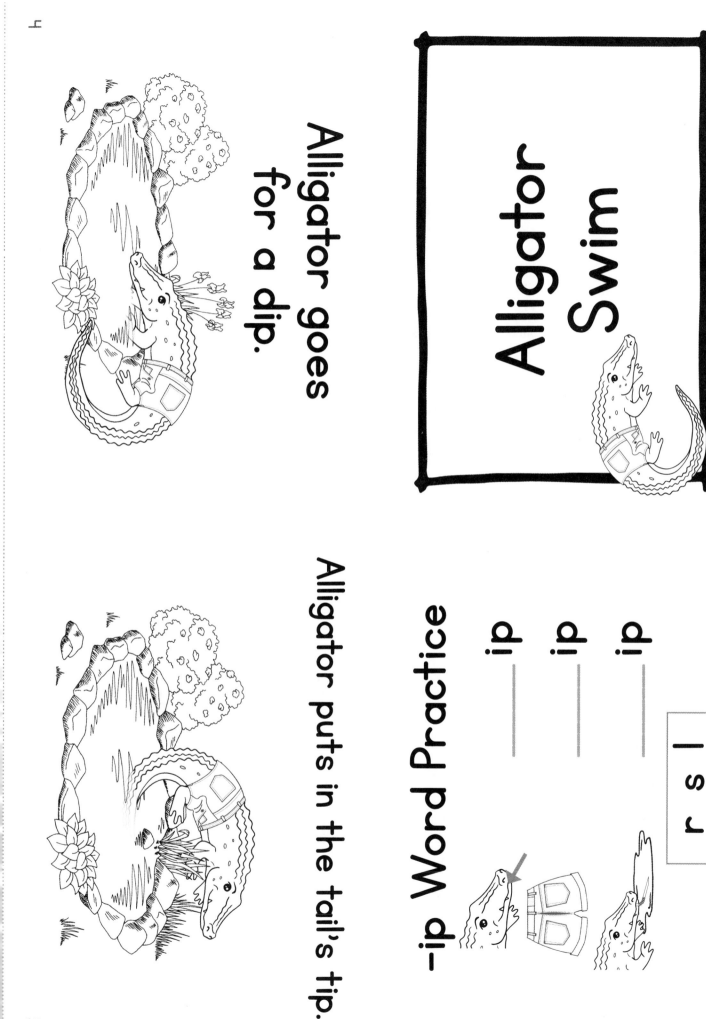

Alligator takes a sip.

The water is on
Alligator's lip.

Alligator hears the
shorts go rip!

It is too cold. Alligator's
body goes flip.

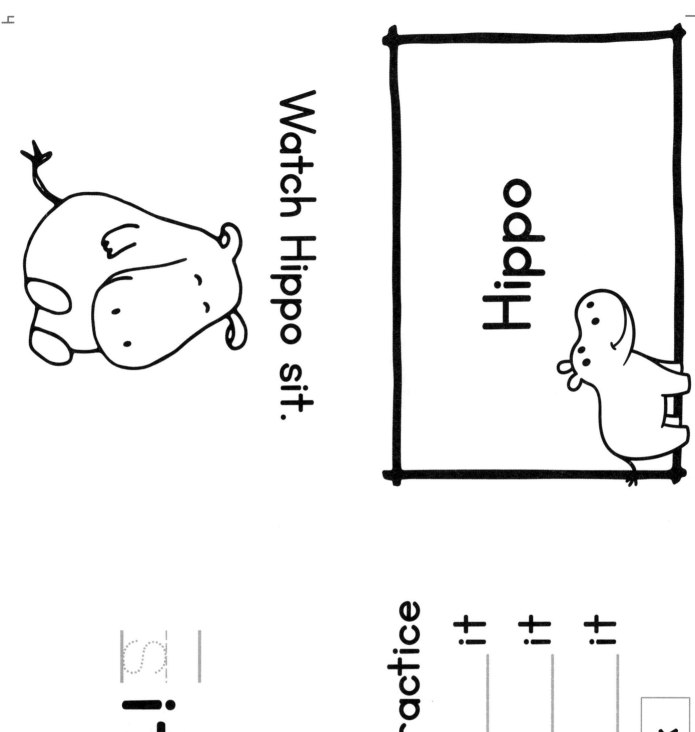

Hippo

Watch Hippo sit.

-it Word Practice

it

it

it

p b k

p d b

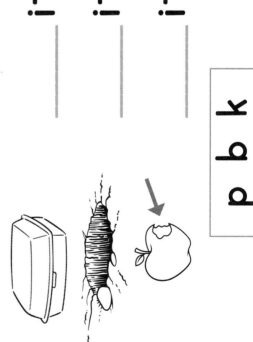

it

sit

Hippo finds a kit.

Hippo bit.

Hippo sits in a pit.

Will Hippo fit?

Kangaroo hops
on a mop.

Kangaroo
Hops

Kangaroo hops
on a top.

-op Word Practice

___ op

___ op

___ op

t	m	p

do

Zebra tells
Kangaroo, "Stop!"

Stop!

Watch Kangaroo hop.

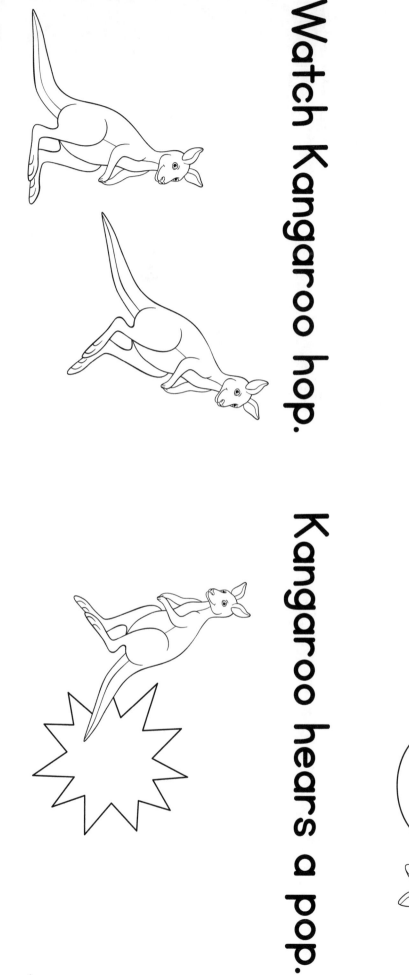

Kangaroo hears a pop.

Giraffe's Spots

Giraffe sees a spot.

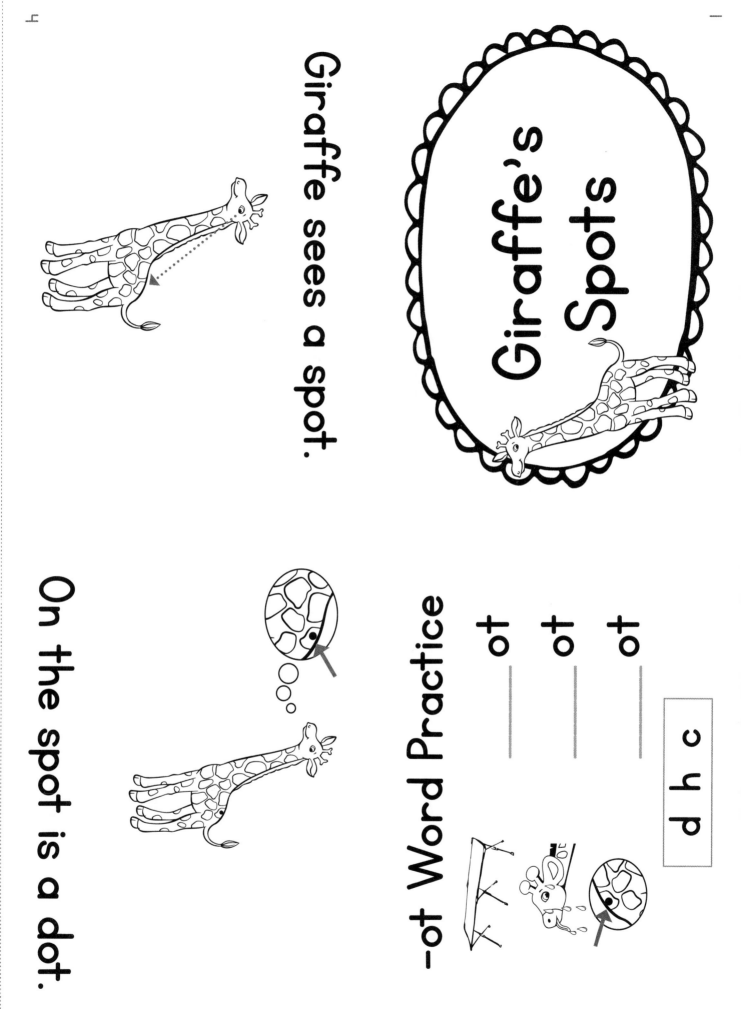

On the spot is a dot.

-ot Word Practice

ot _____

ot _____

to _____

c h p

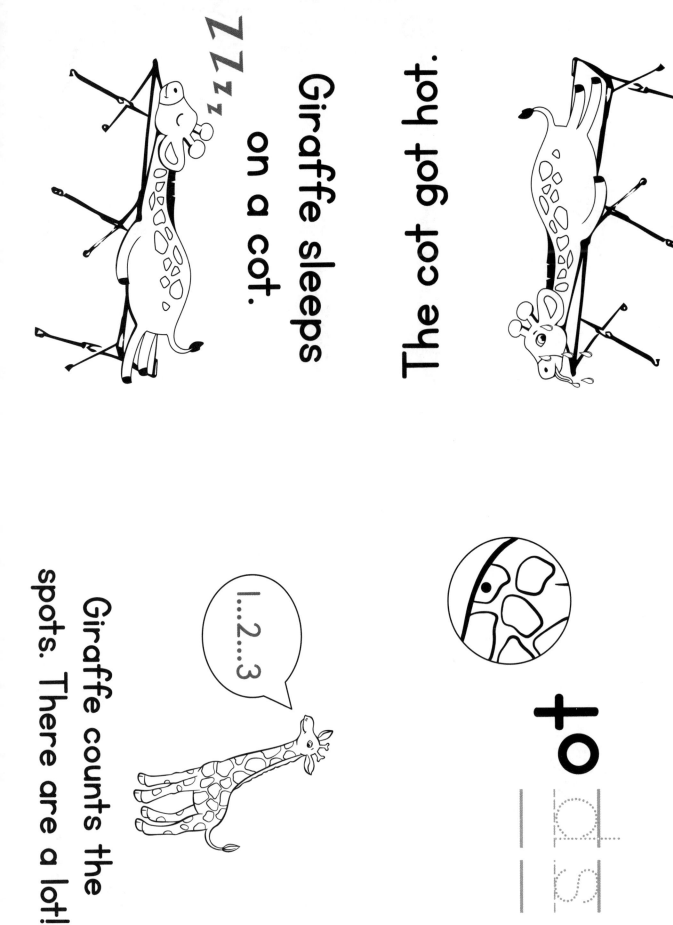

Giraffe sleeps
on a cot.

The cot got hot.

to
ts

Giraffe counts the
spots. There are a lot!

1...2...3

Scrub, scrub, scrub.

Clean Cub

scrub

ub

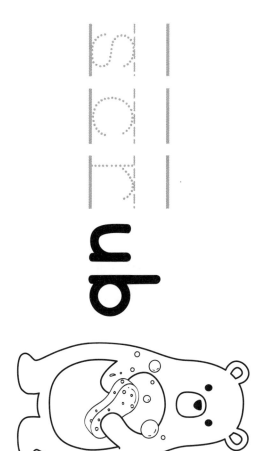

-ub Word Practice

____ub

____ub

____ub

r t c

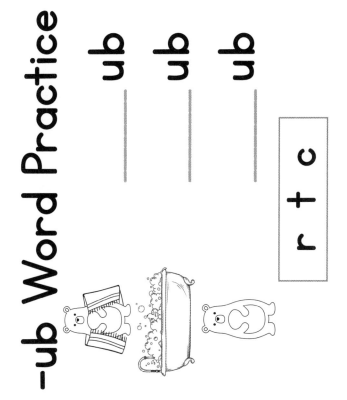

I see the cub.

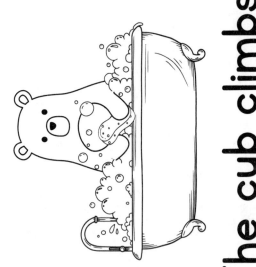

The cub climbs
in the tub.

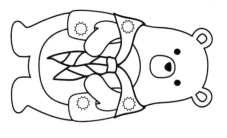

The cub is ready for
the nature club.

Rub, rub, rub.

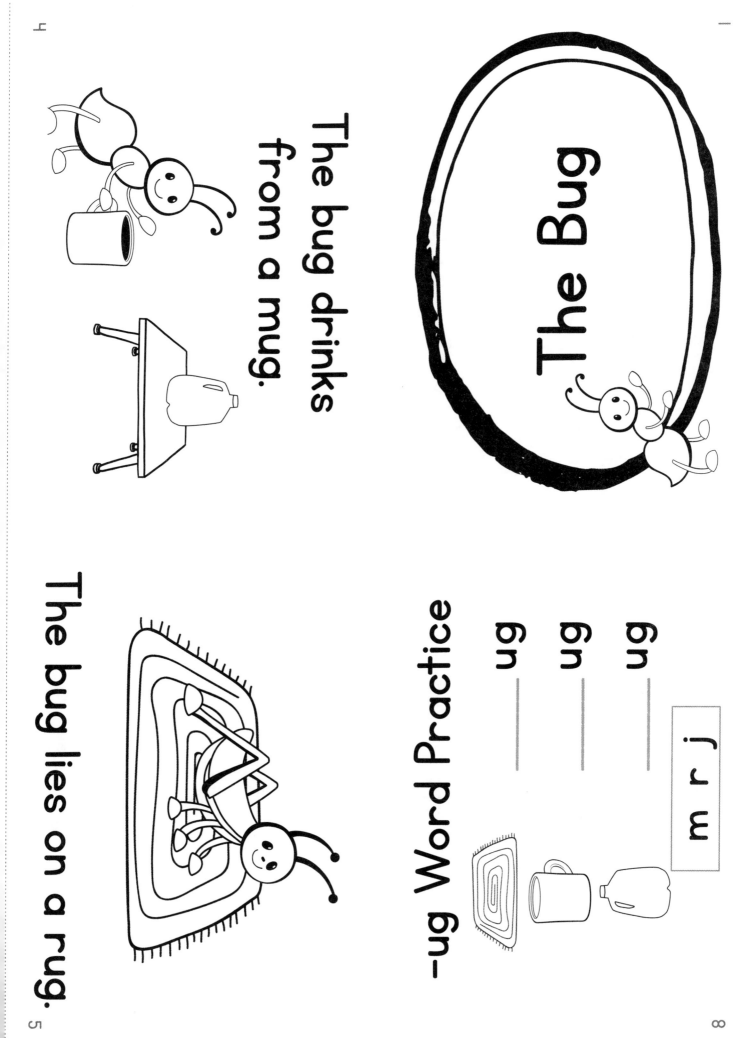

The bug drinks
from a mug.

The Bug

The bug lies on a rug.

-ug- Word Practice

___ug

___ug

___ug

m r j

The bug pulls out the jug.

The bug goes tug.

The bug is snug on the rug.

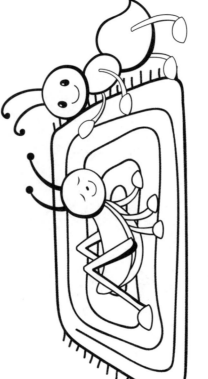

The bug asks for a hug.

cut

ut

A Squirrel

A squirrel feels a
grumble in its gut.

-ut Word Practice

_____ ut

_____ ut

h n

A squirrel pushes the door until it is shut.

A squirrel lives in a hut.

t u

Time to go look for a nut!

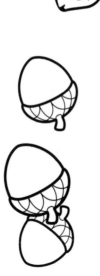

Snail rides on a sail.

Snail Mail

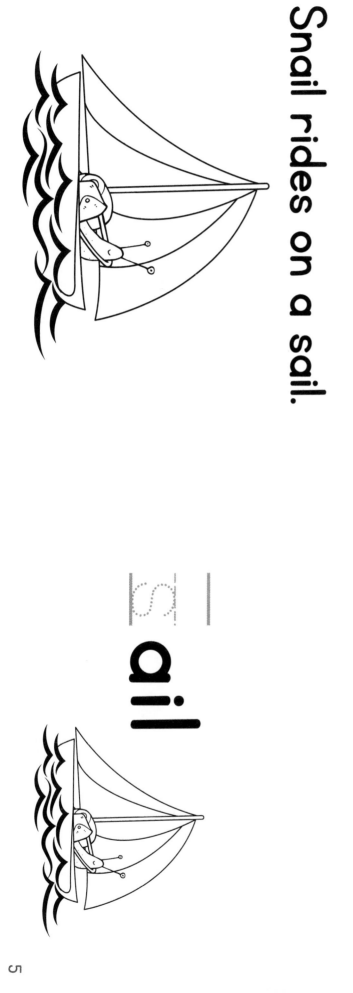

s ail

-ail Word Practice

ail
_____

ail
_____

ail
_____

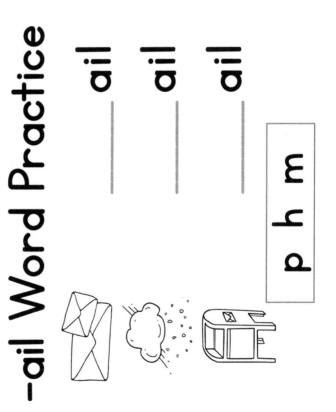

p h m

Snail walks by a tail.

Snail walks
through hail.

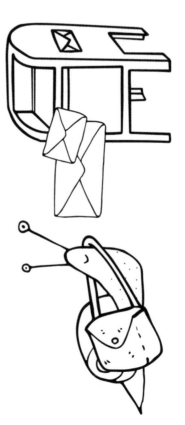

Snail puts mail
in the pail.

Snail delivered
the mail!

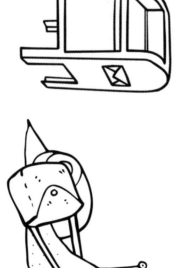

Will Snake bake a rake?

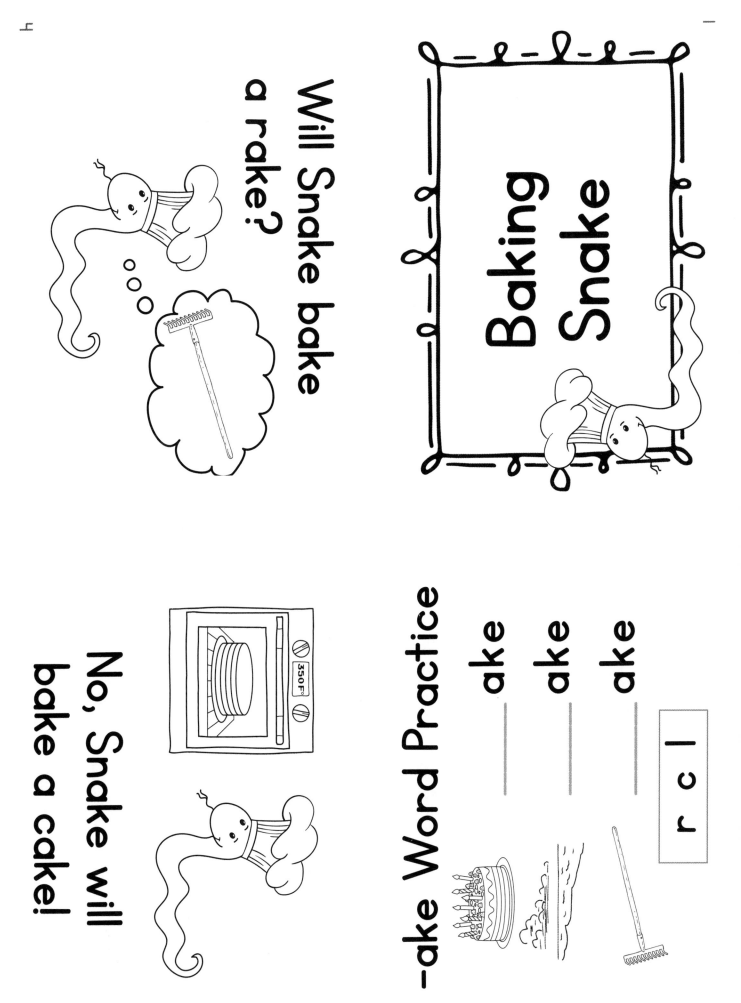

Baking Snake

No, Snake will bake a cake!

-ake Word Practice

___ ake

___ ake

___ ake

r c l

What will
Snake make?

Snake will bake.

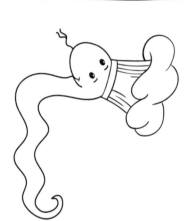

Snake takes the
cake to the lake.

Snake eats cake
with Jake.

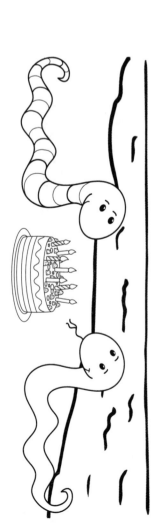

-ang

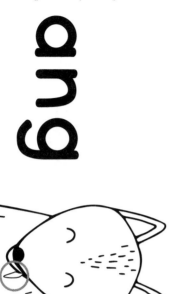

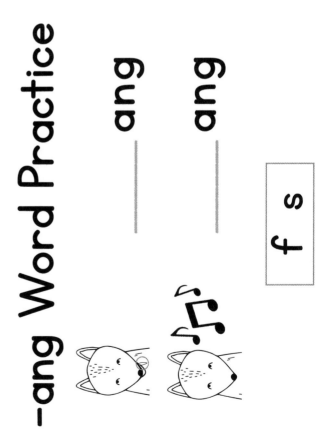

The Wolf's Fang

The wolf pulls the fang with a bang!

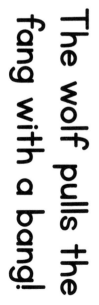

Bang!

-ang Word Practice

_____ ang

_____ ang

s f

Look at that
fang hang.

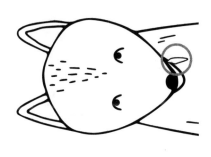

Look at the
wolf's fang.

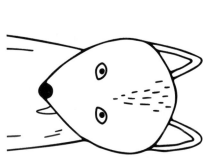

"No more fang,"
the wolf sang!

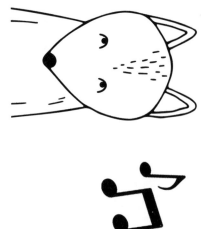

Bang!

fang

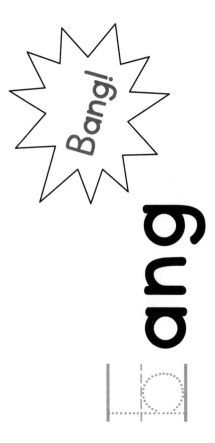

Mark sees a lark.

l ark

Mark at the Park

-ark Word Practice

_____ark

_____ark

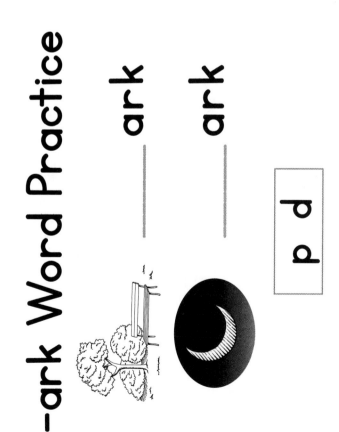

l p

I see a dog named Mark.

Mark goes to the park.

The park gets dark.

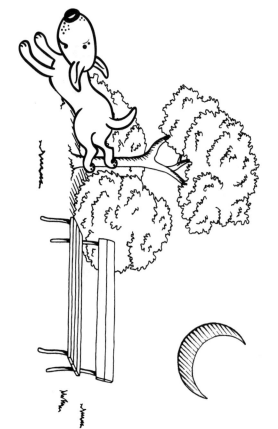

Bark!

The Deer

The deer ate.

The deer ate at
a fast rate.

-ate Word Practice

___ate

___ate

g
p

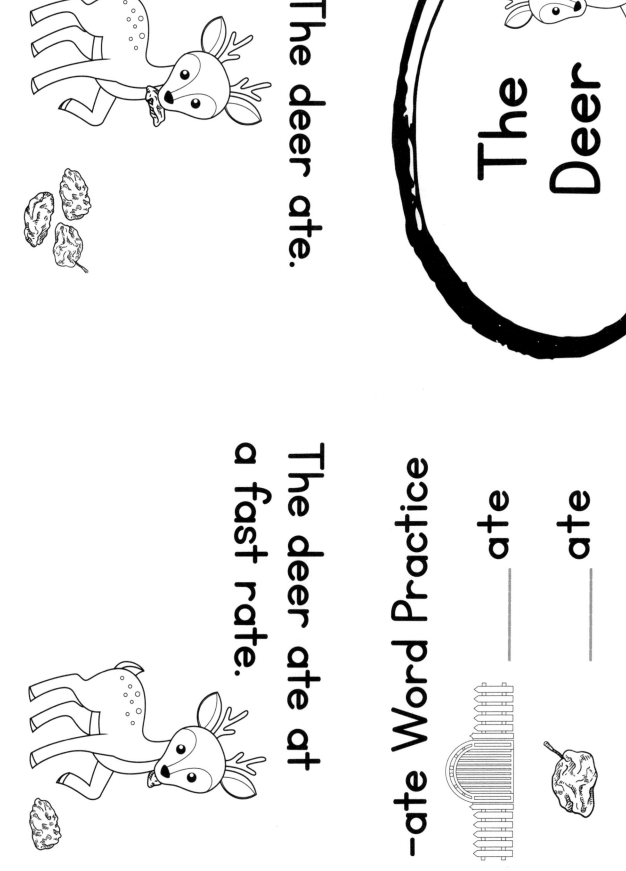

Outside the gate
was a date.

The deer opened
the gate.

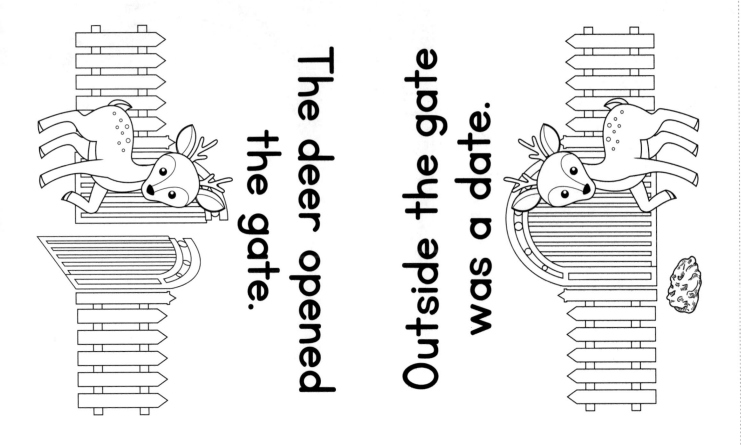

Oh, no! The deer
was late.

D ate

I ate

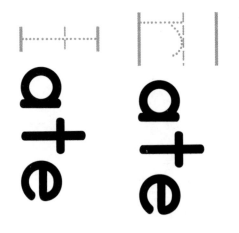

It hit the turtle's shell.

The Turtle

It made the turtle yell!

OW!

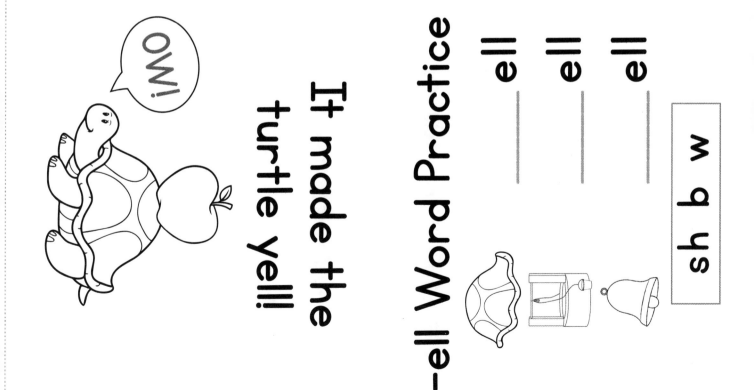

-ell Word Practice

___ell

___ell

___ell

sh b w

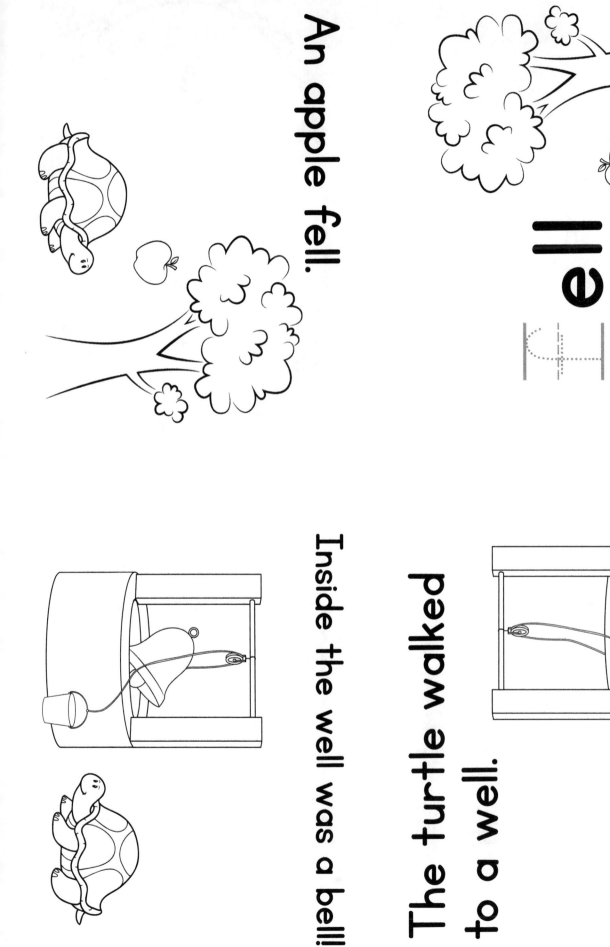

An apple fell.

Fell

Fell

The turtle walked to a well.

Inside the well was a bell!

The mice are nice.

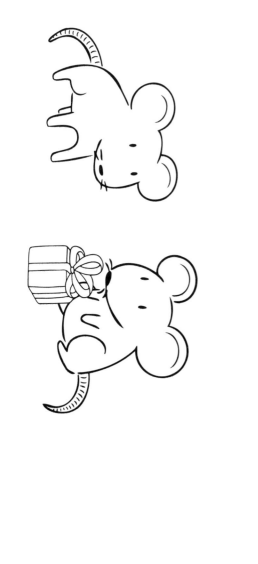

ice

The Three Mice

-ice Word Practice

ice ___

ice ___

ice ___

r	p	m

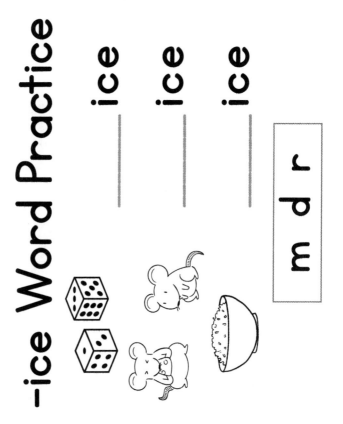

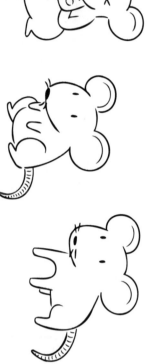

Look at the mice.

The nice mice
eat some rice.

There are three mice.

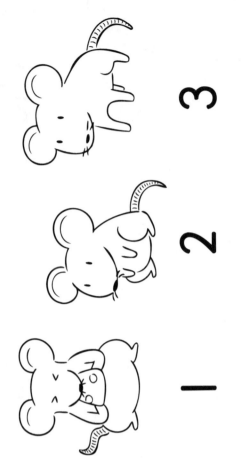

3

2

1

They play with dice.

The Cheetah

Will the cheetah play
with Nick or Rick?

Whom will the cheetah pick?

-ick Word Practice

____ick

____ick

p s

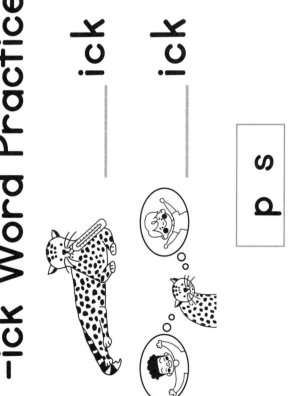

The cheetah feels sick.

The cheetah will feel better quick.

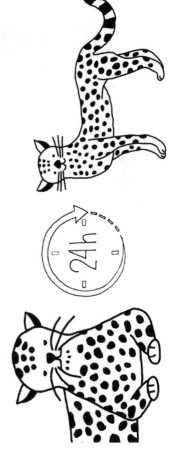

The cheetah gives Nick a lick.

lick

b
il
ill

What Do You See?

Duck says, "Look at my bill!"

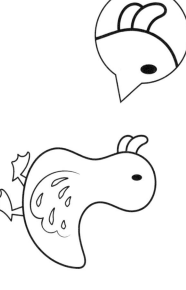

-ill Word Practice

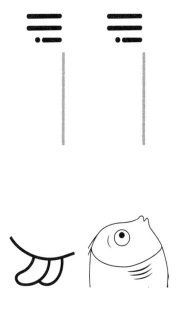

___ill

___ill

b d

Fish says, "Look at my gill!"

Hedgehog says, "Look at my quill!"

ill

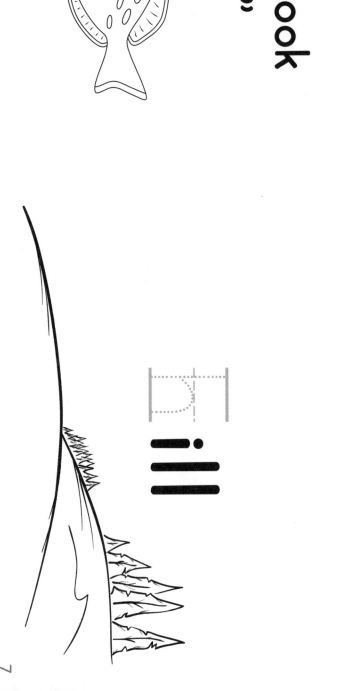

Together, they all walk up the hill.

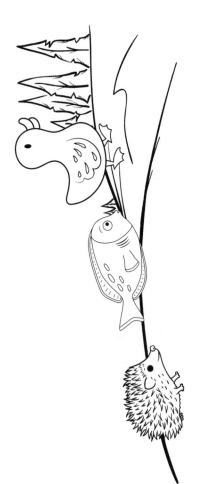

The big ring
is on the
king's wing.

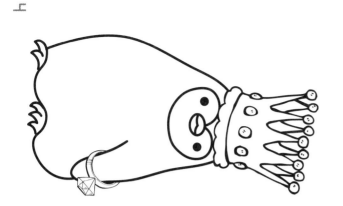

King
Penguin

He rings his
bell with
a ding.

-ing Word Practice

ing
_____

ing
_____

ing
_____

k r p

The king
wears a
big ring.

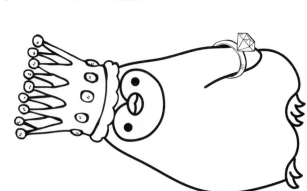

Penguin is a king.

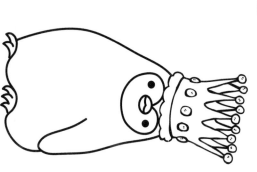

ing

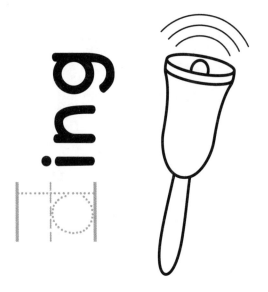

King Penguin wants
someone to sing.

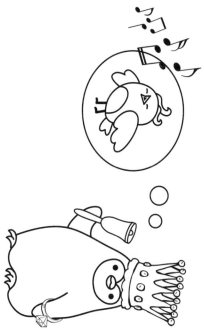

A Fish's Wish

-ish Word Practice

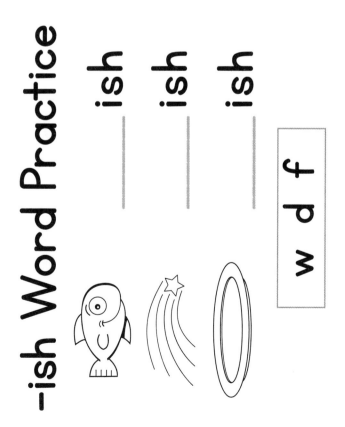

ish

ish

ish

w	f	p

The fish makes a wish.

ish

W

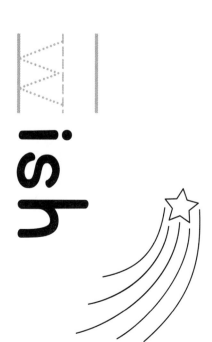

In the bowl is a fish.

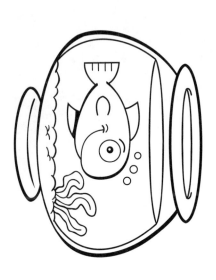

Fish

Fish

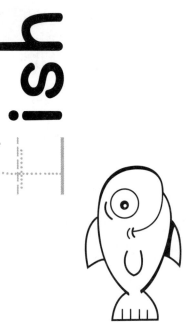

The fish wishes for a dish.

B ock

ock

The Zebra

Zebra asks for
his sock.

-ock Word Practice

_____ ock

_____ ock

_____ ock

s l r

Zebra sees the lock.

Knock, knock, knock.

Zebra trips on a rock.

Zebra makes it
to the dock.

This flamingo
hits a gong.

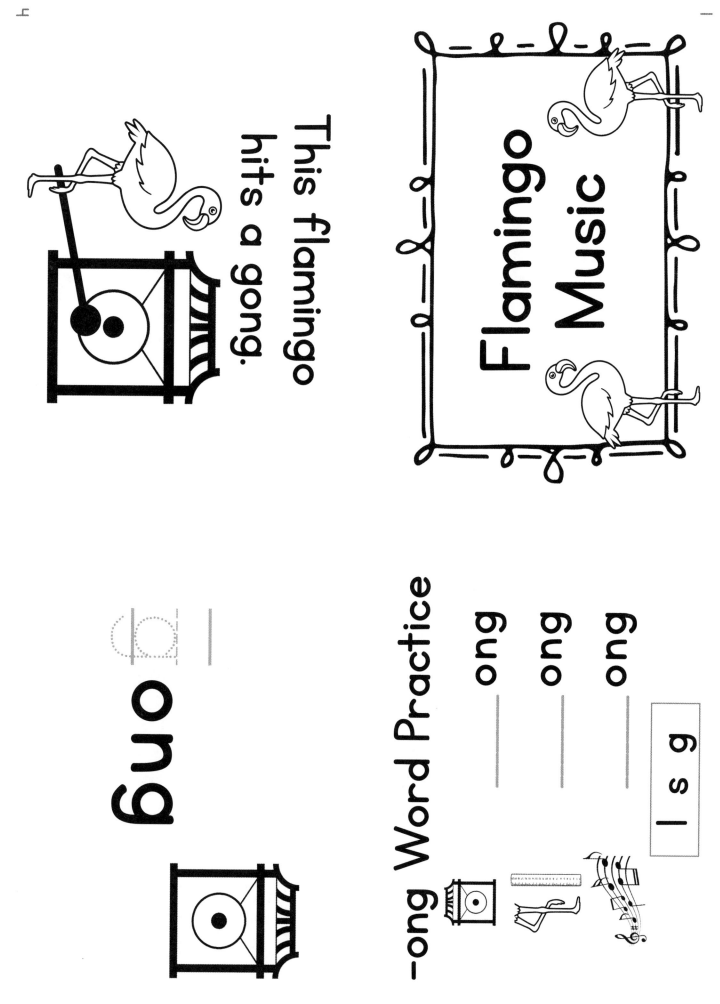

Flamingo
Music

ong

ong

-ong Word Practice

_____ ong

_____ ong

_____ ong

l s g

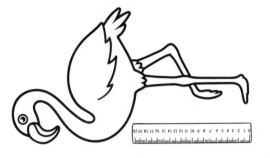

l ong

The flamingo's
legs are so long.

ong

This flamingo
sings a song.

s ong

ight

B e

Owl flies to the right.

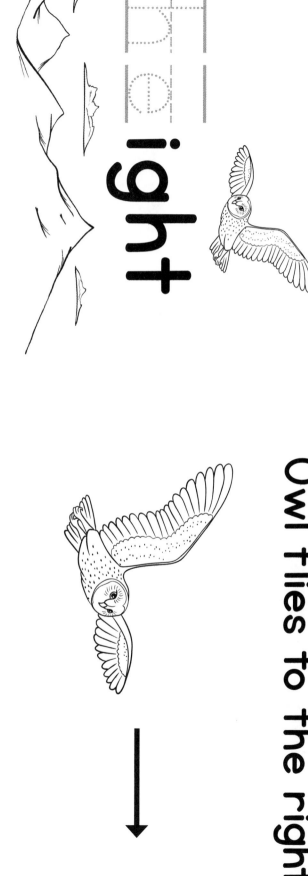

The Owl

-ight Word Practice

___ight

___ight

___ight

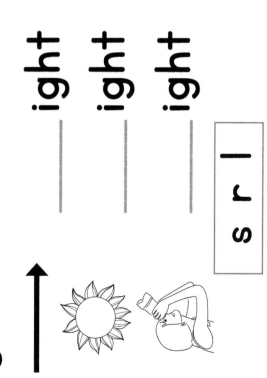

s r l

Owl flies at night.

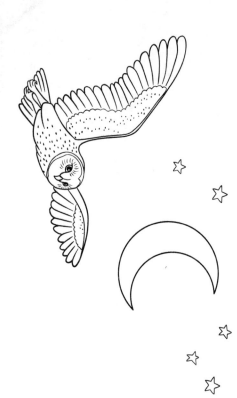

Owl flies at a
great height.

What a sight!

Owl flies until
it is light.

ACKNOWLEDGMENTS

To my love and partner in life: thank you for all of your continued support throughout this entire process. Your ability to always have emotional space and time in your day to look at my progress and celebrate my victories has given me renewed confidence throughout this experience. I appreciate your support making my childhood dreams of being an author an actual reality.

To my family: all of those late nights in school of having you edit my papers and tweak my words to have them be my best is something that I wouldn't change for the world. Your constructive criticism has allowed me to get to this stage of publishing my second workbook, and I couldn't be more grateful for the time that has been invested from each and every one of you. Thank you for always pushing me to do the thing that is a challenge and for never allowing me to settle for the "easy way." This success was only possible because of you.

To past teachers and educators: I want to thank those teachers in my life who showcased my writing, took the time to look at my creations, or told me I could accomplish anything I set my mind to. I am forever grateful for your passion and the way that it has influenced my adult life and career.

ABOUT THE AUTHOR

Celeste Meiergerd is a self-contained special education preschool teacher located in Phoenix, Arizona. After graduating from Arizona State University in 2015 with her bachelor of arts in early childhood education and certification in special education, she began her teaching career. She has worked with a wide range of students, from two to five years of age, all displaying needs in the areas of communication, cognition, social-emotional regulation, adaptive skills, and motor abilities.

Student success is the driving force behind each thing she commits to in her career, as she hopes to inspire young minds in each of her endeavors. This is her second workbook, which follows *The Cars, Trucks, Trains, and Planes Pre-K Workbook*.